MONEY MINDSET SHIFT

Uncover Your Hidden Money Blocks To Get and Keep the Riches You Deserve

Linda Christensen, PhD

© 2015 by Linda Christensen
All Rights Reserved

Success Power Books
Vancouver, BC, Canada

First Printing, 2015
Printed in the United States of America

DISCLAIMER

No portion of this material is intended to offer legal, medical, personal or financial advice. The information contained herein cannot replace or substitute for the services of trained professionals in any field, including financial, legal or therapeutic matters. Under no circumstances, including but not limited to negligence, will Linda Christensen be liable for any special or consequential damages that result from the use of, or the inability to use, the material, information or strategies communicated through these materials, or any services following these materials, even if advised of the possibility of such damages.

TERMS OF USE

No part of this publication may be reproduced or transmitted in any form or by any means, mechanical or electronic, including photocopying and recording, or by any information storage and retrieval system, without permission in writing from the author (except by a reviewer, who may quote brief passages).

© 2015 All Rights Reserved
Linda Christensen, PhD

Table of Contents

Introduction 7
Chapter 1: Why I Wrote This Book 9
Chapter 2: Why You Must Read This Book 19

Part I: Understanding Money and You 25
Chapter 3: Money Makes the World Go Round!....... 27
Chapter 4: The World Is A Changin' 31
Chapter 5: What Is Money Anyways? 37
Chapter 6: What Does Money Mean To You? 43
Chapter 7: Money Mindset: ....
 _It's all just in your head!............................. 47

Part II: Uncovering Your Money Blocks 53
Chapter 8: Money Block #1 - Fear......................... 55
Chapter 9: Money Block #2 - Social Conditioning ... 61
Chapter 10: Money Block #3 - Woundings.............. 71
Chapter 11: Money Block #4 - ....
 __Low Self-Worth 75
Chapter 12: Money Block #5 - Money Chaos........... 81
Chapter 13: What This All Adds Up To Is 87
Chapter 14: So What's Your Story Going To Be?..... 91
Chapter 15: About The Author............................... 97

Introduction

CHAPTER ONE

Why I Wrote This Book

I'm concerned.

In fact, I hate to say it…I'm worried.

About you. About the future. About my son. And everyone else's kids. About many baby-boomers like me who've suffered serious, unexpected financial setbacks.

The world has changed dramatically since I was a kid. It was a breeze to get a job, to find a nice place to live, to do whatever I wanted. Never had any debt. And a sense of so many possibilities for the future.

Things are different now. As a college professor I get students coming to me, asking if it's worth it to get a degree with so much debt when there aren't any jobs out there. We've all heard about those cab drivers with PhD's. Our education system is faltering and not preparing the youth for the real world.

It's not just young people who are facing challenges. Many of us born in the fifties and sixties, have become disillusioned about getting ahead financially…getting laid off in our fifties, being wiped out through a divorce or bankruptcy, and just not having enough pension for those "golden years." As the older generation struggles with their dreams being broken, the younger generation struggles with having any dreams for the future.

Whether young or old, challenges exist in our volatile times. The question to be raised is…are you able to handle them?

Life Is A Dance
There are two key dynamics at play in our dance with life. The **outer** world of circumstances. Our **inner** world of mindset and core, deep seated beliefs.

Financial disaster hits when the two collide.

When outer challenges meet inner limitations we crash.

You see there are a lot of people out there who are really messed up in terms of mindset but manage to get through life by maintaining an easy enough job with security...like most government jobs. But if that were taken away they'd be in crisis.

Then there are those who are in a place of mastery in their inner game. When challenges show up in terms of getting laid off, going bankrupt or getting sued, they rise up again into success.

That's why I'm worried.

The outer world of circumstances is becoming more challenging...and people's mindsets have in many ways deteriorated. Thanks to the entitlement mentality that's become acculturated.

More people are crashing.

We seriously need to master our inner game if we want not just to *survive* but *thrive* in the future. That inner game is about mindset and beliefs, but it goes deeper than that.

It's really all about *energy*.

A mindset is the **outer**, more visible form of an **inner** energy pattern at work. To shift our relationship with money is about shifting those energetic patterns *behind* our beliefs and behaviours.

This is the secret to lasting transformation.

Change your energy, change your life.

Likewise, if you change your outer behaviours and beliefs, you change those energy patterns. It goes both ways. They're interconnected. You can change from the inside out and from the outside in.

Now I had to learn all of this the hard way. As always, life is our master teacher.

How I Got Sucked Into Poverty Consciousness

I gradually got ensnared into a poverty consciousness during my marriage. The seeds planted in me as a child of not being worthy and deserving got activated during these years to blossom into a life of ongoing deprivation. The more I tolerated and accepted negative experiences, the more I got entangled in an energetic web of **lack**. I was always willing to "tough it out" and hang in there. I didn't expect anything more or better…I just wished for it.

Remember this.

You get in life what you *expect* to get. Not what you just *wish* for.

To illustrate this a bit I'll describe where I lived.

You know that your environment has a profound effect on shaping who you *feel* you are. And I purposely say *feel* for that is at your core, your subconscious, whereas what you *think*, your conscious mind, tends to cover the deeper truth with rationalizations.

My husband decided to buy this "cheap" cabin on an Indian reserve where we had only wood for heat and that was with this home-made stove contraption underneath the cabin that I could only access through a dirt crawlspace to put wood in the stove. Of course, I had to first dry and chop the wood so it was burnable. Then it would only last for an hour and I'd have to crawl in there again.

I always had dirty nails and wore grubby clothes. Believe me, as a woman your self-esteem drops pretty low in those conditions. I'd find myself scraping ice off of the *inside* of the windows and at night I'd go to bed with three layers of clothes on to keep warm.

I'm sure you're thinking…"That sure is stupid! Why on earth did you do that?"

I'd agree. It was stupid. And there's no way I'd put up with that today.

It was my husband's idea to buy this shack and set up the heating system like that. As a good and loyal wife I always gave him the benefit of the doubt. I figured he must know what's best. Something that cost me dearly. Why we didn't put in electric heaters is beyond me. He thought it would be too expensive.

I only first got it that I had become so locked into this poverty consciousness when years later, after I left my husband, I was at a Toastmaster's Meeting. Someone else was asked what their worst Christmas present was. So that got me to think what mine would have been…then I remembered.

One Christmas I got three used candles from my husband.

I had totally forgot about it.

Money Mindset Shift

Then and there it really hit me! How I had gotten so used to being deprived, always tolerating so much misery, I didn't expect anything much better than that. I longed for better things, yes, but I continued to passively accept my impoverished circumstances.

So…how could this have happened?

It's not like I came from a poor family. In fact, my father was a very successful businessman. He immigrated here from Germany after the war, having lost everything, his home, business and family all killed and everything was taken from him. He worked, saved enough money to buy a building to start his own bakery. Over the years with the money he made he bought over two sections of land to build a ranch, with over 400 head of cattle. Built a beautiful home on an acreage outside of Calgary, Alberta and eventually retired and moved to Scottsdale, Arizona. So what's the catch? How did I get into this negative web of deprivation?

Well…let's explore that a bit.

The Factors At Play That Set Me Up For Poverty

I was extremely naive in my younger years.

Not raised in a religious home I had a profound spiritual experience which led me to commit to the spiritual path at 18. In my mind that meant I was to abandon all concern for material goals and renounce any material desires.

Right here, you can see how certain religious teachings can really mess you up. Beliefs that misdirect you in life. I'll be addressing this later on.

This opened the door to my tolerating rather toxic conditions. You know the line, that *life's struggles and hardships are meant to teach you lessons*, how to be unselfish and sacrifice yourself for higher causes and other people…that this is the required path of spiritual growth.

To add to this, I tend to be pretty tough and can endure a lot (I'm a Scorpio with my moon in Taurus). I hate to wimp out at anything and don't back down in front of challenges. My strength as a virtue can be my downfall. It justified my toleration…"Hey, I'm strong, I can handle this." (But why should you is another question!)

I'm also very loyal. I loved my husband with my whole heart and soul. I was willing to go through thick and thin, no matter what. And so I did until I lost faith in him. I gave him the extra 1000 miles until I could no longer believe in him.

Yes, I was continually disappointed and not happy about things. Not living the way I really wanted to. (The situation wasn't just about poverty but also some pretty extreme social alienation. These days I socially interact with people more in one week than I did in a whole year.)

In "being spiritual" I always reasoned that I'm the one that's not happy here, he was okay with it all, therefore there must be something wrong with me. I am the problem. I need to fix myself. I've got to be responsible for my own happiness. And so I deeply got into a lot of personal growth work. This led to highlighting our differences. I was choosing a different life trajectory of on-going growth and self-awareness which wasn't being shared.

A huge stumbling block for me was how I *over spiritualized* all of this. I regularly told myself that these challenges were for me to learn unconditional love. To use every circumstance as an opportunity to develop myself, to become bigger and greater than the circumstances. I so believed that if only I became more spiritual I could transcend whatever physical or emotional limitations and challenges life would divvy out to me and be able to live in this state of enlightened bliss, no matter what.

Now I have to say that my approach did a lot for me in terms of how I grew and developed as a person. In the big picture I am a better, wiser, stronger person for all of this. But…was it really necessary to go through almost 20 years of misery for this? I don't think so. It took a lot of misery to get me to question a lot of my assumptions about what being spiritual is all about. It actually came down to a matter of life or death for me.

I had so struggled with not being happy in this relationship for about 19 years, that I had no energy, was feeling sick without actually being sick, to the point that I was worried if I could keep working.

I came to realize that I was living a life of on-going self-betrayal. For me to continue in this situation was like I was saying "No" to *my life*. It hit me one day that I had to commit to saying a big "Yes" to *me*. I just knew that if I stayed in this marriage I'd be getting cancer or something, and be staying on a path that would lead to death. But the catch in all of this is that he often was suicidal. He threatened to kill himself many a time and especially if he thought I'd leave him.

So I had to make a choice. The ultimate choice.

My life or his.

I had to say "Yes" to me, to my life, to what I wanted and how I wanted to live. No matter what. And to stop sacrificing myself to keep him happy. And so I left. (Don't worry, he's still alive too).

Linda Christensen, PhD

The Seed That Sprouted Into Deprivation

What really allowed for all this at a deeper level is this core belief I had. That "it's okay for Linda to be deprived and not valued." You see, these beliefs aren't really conscious. It's not like you go around saying that to yourself all day. In "being spiritual" I stopped the negative self-talk on the conscious level but underneath that the energy of low self-worth was still operating in my subconscious. That's why this can be so tricky.

You see at home growing up I didn't get much (hardly any) affirmation or any real attention. I don't think my mother ever asked me how I was. I never felt anyone in my family ever knew me. I never felt safe to actually share my thoughts and feelings. This translates into the message that I'm not worth listening to or getting to know.

That's why I fell in love with my husband.

He cared enough to listen and know me, and made me feel safe to share myself with him. I was received. (To make it clear, he is a wonderful man with so many terrific qualities and huge potential. That's why I stayed with him and loved him for as long as I did.)

Here lay the seed that under the right conditions would grow into a garden of "poverty consciousness." A deep, largely unconscious, sense of not feeling worthy or deserving of anything better than deprivation and neglect.

You see, the way I've come to look at it is that we all have various seeds of potential within us. Some can become the weeds of poverty and others can sprout magnificent trees of abundance. **The choices we make in the face of various circumstances serve to activate, nurture and cultivate particular seeds.**

Seeds that otherwise lie dormant, awaiting their opening to actualize their potential.

So our lives are like a garden. We actively and consciously need to *weed out* the negative beliefs. The stories that disempower us and give us excuses not to step into our greatness. And then we need to proactively *plant and nurture* the seeds of creativity, joy, abundance, and success.

It's been a journey to get over all this. I had to rethink how spirituality relates to success and money. How it is that we can get stuck in a poverty consciousness and how to get out of it. What really are the keys to a success mindset and what are its obstacles. And, of course, what does it really mean to be spiritual and take up a "spiritual path."

In going deeper and deeper into this, I've found it's really all about energy. Our thoughts, feelings, our very being is an expression of energetic patterns. To heal, transform, change ourselves, we need to shift those deeper energetic patterns.

And so I wrote this book.

My hope is that you find this book insightful as to how money, success and *you* function on an energetic level in your life. For the real secret behind success, what it's really all about…is shifting that *energy!* And money is a form of energy.

With blessings and love, to your abundance!
Dr. Linda.

P.S. Remember to get your bonuses! Go to MoneyMindsetShift.com and put in the code MONEYSHIFT.

CHAPTER TWO

Why You Must Read This Book

I've got news for you....You've been lied to.
Money *DOES* buy happiness!

Money is the ticket to FREEDOM. With it you'll be able to do, be, and have whatever you want.

If you had all the money in the world...you could have the best personal trainers, the best diet advice, the best doctors and health products, the best therapists, the best gurus, the best cosmetic surgeons...all at your side serving you!

You could travel wherever and whenever you'd want! Have the adventure of a lifetime...over and over again! Have those nice clothes, eat out in nice restaurants and order the best wine with the best desserts.

It's not about gluttony...although some may get trapped in that.

It's about being able to appreciate and enjoy, experience and celebrate, all the wonders and beauty that life has to offer. It's about living life to the max! With gratitude and appreciation. To gratefully receive and honour this tremendous, priceless, gift of life.

When you're well off you have the blessed opportunity to engage life fully when *poverty* and *being broke* isn't holding you back!

Just think of all the things you can't do because "I can't afford it".... Nothing steals happiness faster than poverty!

The Great Invitation for You!

Life is there holding out its hand to you, inviting you to receive its many gifts...and you can't take it on because you don't have the money.

I'm out to have a blast at this game called Life. I want to die with no regrets, feeling satiated that I "sucked the marrow out of life." That means many things.

For me it's to experience the beauty and wonder of life in its many facets and to also know that I make the world a better place. To be fulfilled in life involves having contributed to it in serving others in some way.

So what can this book do for you to get you on the path to your most awesome life?
- Shift your mindset about money.
- Change your very being in terms of how you operate in the world.
- Transform your energetic signature to one that is receptive to and in resonance with wealth.
- Birth a new energetic contract that's saying a big "YES" to life and money!
- Bring you into Money Mastery!

How This Works

You see you'll find two people in the same area, same background, in the same business...one succeeds and the other doesn't. You can have people with great talent who remain poor, and those with little talent becoming rich. You can have serious economic downturns, like the great depression where more millionaires were made than any other time until recently. You can have the degrees, the knowledge, the opportunities…and still…just not make it in this world.

So what's truly the difference between the successful and the wannabe's…the winners and the losers?….it's not what most people think.

It's about your inner game
so you can see success in your outer game.

The external conditions of the world are not the ultimate determining factor. It's really about our state of being and how we operate. It's about energy and knowing how to shift it. That's where the real change and work has to happen, along with taking the right action in the right sequence.

Many call this your mindset, others call it your success principles, and then some say it's all about the Law of Attraction. They're all true. It's about your deeper, largely subconscious beliefs, that govern your state of being which constitute a type of energetic signature, a pattern of energy that reflects the patterns of beliefs that direct our patterns of behaviours. This is one's "deep self" or energetic self that often is a mystery to us. We so focus on the obvious, the seen, the material self and our conscious beliefs. And then we wonder why we screw up so much. We procrastinate and self-sabotage. We experience ongoing frustration and struggle.

What's going on is that there's the conscious part of us saying "let's go this way" while our deeper subconscious self is saying "nope, we're going that way." Guess what? The subconscious is more powerful and wins.

Now that's why I wrote this book! There's not much out there that addresses these *deeper dynamics* at work in our relationship to money.

What We'll Cover In This Book

To set up the context for all this we first look at what money is all about in **Part I: Understanding Money and You.** First by looking at how central money is in our lives and what it actually represents. Then we look at how the world is changing and how we need to embrace a new paradigm of what I call *Sacred Abundance* (Chapters 3-5). Then in Chapters 6 and 7 you're led to explore what money means to you! Here you start creating a list of some beliefs that might be messing things up for you.

Then we go on to address specific money blocks in **Part II: Uncover Your Money Blocks.** We'll look at five key areas where we tend to have a subconscious belief and energetic pattern in place that's blocking abundance and success from our lives (Chapters 8-12). The first being fear, followed by various beliefs, what I call "syndromes," that we've picked up through social conditioning. Then we have "life woundings" where certain negative experiences shape how we relate to money, followed by issues of low self-worth, and finally there's what I call "money chaos." (A lack of practical money management which often results from the previous four issues. So for example, when we're afraid of money, or don't believe we're deserving, we self-sabotage in neglecting our finances.)

I show how these all add up to a particular ***energetic contract*** we've got in place in Chapter 13. Our unique combination of subconscious beliefs are wrapped up into ***stories*** that function like a contract we've entered into and are then living out of. The result is that we are manifesting this energetic pattern of lack, struggle and failure, instead of success and abundance.

How To Use This Book

I want this book to change your life. To launch you on your path to wealth and success. To set you free from whatever's holding you back.

That's why I've included in here some exercises for you to address your particular money blocks. So get out your journal and pen and please DO the exercises as you read.

So it's time to say good-bye to any and all excuses.

Read this book and start owning your money power. Realize this:

***When you master money,
you'll master your life.***

Are you ready for that? All right then, let's get rockin'… and look at why this is such an important issue.

Don't forget you get an audio version with this. Just go to MoneyMindsetShift.com and put in the code MONEYSHIFT to access it.

Part I

Understanding Money and You

CHAPTER THREE

Money Makes the World Go Round!

We need to take a little look here as to how important money is in our lives. It's so central to our lives yet we so neglect it!

Money Dictatorship!
Just imagine going through your typical day.
You get out of the bed you bought, along with its sheets and your PJs…you go to the bathroom in the place you rent or bought, brush your teeth with the toothbrush you bought…then go to make your coffee, breakfast…you know, the food you bought…get dressed, get in your car…all of which you bought…to go to work to earn the money…so you can buy all of the above!

After work you go for a drink and appy's with friends, home for dinner, then to a movie…all of which you bought…after some years at a college to get qualified for your job…which cost a few grand….

Then, when your forties and fifties come around you start hoping to have enough saved for retirement some day so you don't have to work for that money but still somehow, magically, have it coming in so you're not one of those homeless hobos on the street.

Get the gist? Your whole life revolves around money!

Every day…virtually every transaction…involves the getting and giving of money.

We pretty much spend our whole life on getting that money and then spending it just to be able to survive and function.

It dominates our lives! We live under a type of *Money Dictatorship*. Really let that sink in. Pretty crazy isn't it?

Hey Money! Let's Connect Sometime!

Here comes the irony. Now more than ever we're seriously disconnected from our money even though it's so central and dominant in our lives. Why? Because we hardly ever touch and see the stuff!

Everything is automated. We don't see our money coming in as cash or pay checks anymore, it's all automatically deposited into our bank accounts. We don't see our money going out, as our bills are on auto-pay. Then, when we go shopping we use our debit or credit cards.

We hardly ever use cash.

So what's the impact of all this? Well ask yourself these questions:
- Can you say exactly what you get paid?
- How much is taken off for taxes?
- What your expenses were in the past month?
- Exactly what you owe on all your credit cards?

I bet you anything if you actually received cash for your work and could only use cash for everything you'd buy you'd be way more attentive of your money and less eager to let go of it!

Being so disconnected from our money today is one big reason why there's so much debt.

This is something that needs to be "healed"...which means to be made whole, brought back into integration, reconnected.

What we need is to get really connected with our money *emotionally* but in a *healthy* way.

To get connected emotionally is actually to create a love relationship with money. To give it the attention and nurturing you would to your lover. This bond of love will create an energetic contract where money will love you in return and stick with you. Just like a marriage, as you commit and are faithful to money, money will return the loyalty and devotion!

This is what many are calling these days the Law of Attraction, and becoming a Money Magnet.

But that's not all.

Because of how central money is and how we neglect to create a healthy relationship with it, it can seriously mess up our relationships. Money wreaks havoc for couples.

"Hon'...why can't you make more money?" "Babe...why don't you spend less of it!"

Our unhealthy and unconscious relationship with money causes a lot of friction between couples.

We've all heard it. Financial stress is the #1 cause behind divorce. The thing couples argue the most about is money. It's a big issue. Nothing can make your life more miserable than the constant struggle to keep your head above water.

A survey done at the University of Michigan found that what people worry the most about was money, what makes them the happiest is getting that extra money, and what makes them the most unhappy is not having enough of it. True that not all rich people are happy, but nothing can take away your happiness faster than realizing you just can't pay your bills, you might lose your home or car, and you can't look after your kids.

Of course, there's a balance, of having more than enough, to be free from the stress of money worries, being at peace, happy and fulfilled. There are people who have millions, even billions, and constantly worry about losing it all. Then there are those with just enough moment of not having an empty stomach.

It's relative to one's context. But also, it's about one's mindset…one's beliefs and expectations. Specifically…your money mindset. More on that in a bit.

A quick recap here.

***Money dominates our lives,
yet we're pretty disconnected from it,
but yet we sure worry and fight over it.
Nothing messes up our relationships and
happiness more than money.***

Before we get into our money blocks and mindset let's take a look at how the world of money is changing on a global scale and how we're trying to live in a paradigm that's out of date. We need to wake up to the changing times.

CHAPTER FOUR

The World Is A Changin'

We're in revolutionary times. It's sneaky.

It's a type of revolution that's happening without much political revolt and bloodshed, next to no media attention, but revolutionary nevertheless. The role of global economic dynamics and the impact of the internet on all facets of life.

Once Upon A time...
Most of us are still coasting along in the aftermath of the industrial age. Where America came into wealth and power through the 19th and 20th centuries with the massive production of goods for export.

It's in this context that our public schooling system for the masses was instituted. The purpose being to train a workforce for the manufacturing plants and to serve the businesses of the rich elites.

Unions were born to address the exploitation of the masses. Making sure there'd be lunch breaks, only a 40 hour work week, getting paid for overtime, with vacation and sick pay, and a retirement pension to top it off.

The result is the typical middle class scenario of the perfect family living in the 'burbs with that white picket fence...hubby going to work 9-5...wifey at home looking after the kids, making supper. The ideal life that got put in place in the 1950's which represented the American dream.

That generation was a lucky one to experience the wealth of the times, including a hefty pension that would see retirees through those golden years. And for them they were golden years.

Well...that was so *yesterday* folks.

Let's Time Travel into the Future
Today it's a different story. Pension funds are shaky and will be running dry. The stock markets are highly volatile...crashes seriously depleting the investments people were counting on to see them through those golden years. Seniors are re-entering the workforce...they just can't make ends meet.

People are getting laid off, left, right and centre. More jobs are outsourced with services provided from overseas. Most manufacturing is being done in third world countries for lower wages and minimal benefits.

A huge issue in the works is that the baby boomers seriously outnumber the younger generation that has to carry the financial burden. Not only for the pension of their parents but the insanely high taxes and national debt that has ensued in recent years. Let's face it folks. The American debt of approaching 18 trillion is literally cosmic in nature.

[To put things into perspective...one billion minutes takes us back to the time of Christ. Yes...you read that right. That's just one billion MINUTES! Do you realize how colossal the debt is here? We're living in *la la land* if we think everything's okay.]

We can't afford to be passive and ignorantly blissful about our financial futures. We all think somebody else will take care of it...that the taxes (our government) will pay for our future welfare. But whose taxes? Remember, those wealthy people we think should pay for it all make up only 1%.

Not only is there the issue of massive federal debt...as well as municipal (with some cities on the brink of bankruptcy in the US) there's been an on-going trend of higher personal debt. The younger generation is growing up with credit cards, using them with reckless abandon. It feels like they've got free and easy money in their hands.

Things are looking pretty grim...if one is just passively going along with the status quo.

It's time to wake up
and come into money mastery.

Okay, That Was The Bad News, How About Some Good News!

There is some good news in all of this.

More people are being called into conscious, creative entrepreneurship. It's a new trend, a movement that's happening.

Many want to come into money mastery and own their destiny by starting a business, largely as consultants, coaches, experts operating as solo-entrepreneurs.

Behind this crisis is a fabulous opportunity.

You see we tend to passively go through life, coasting along when things are pretty good. It's when we hit a wall, a crisis, that we then start to question what we're doing. Why? Because it ain't workin' anymore!

It's only in questioning *what is* that we then go on a quest to go *deeper* into life and seek to understand how it works. That results in **wisdom**.

Our consciousness expands, we become more aware, and that opens the door to ***new possibilities***. We grow, we step into our greatness and become bigger in terms of who we are. We activate our creative potential. The saying, "Necessity is the Mother of Invention" comes into play here.

This is how the economic crises we're facing on both a personal and global level can lead to a deep, spiritual awakening! We either transform and get enlightened or collapse.

We can begin our spiritual awakening right here in how we relate to money.

Money Mastery Involves A Shift In Your Energy

I love the saying of T. Harv Eker's "How you do anything, is how you do everything." We can apply this to money…

*How you do money
is how you do everything.*

It's all interrelated. How you fundamentally *relate* to life and yourself, will reflect in how you *relate* to money.

If you *shift* your relationship with money and success in a profound way it will *shift* how you fundamentally relate to yourself and life.

That's the goal of this book. To create a ***shift*** in your being, your very life. That shift is fundamentally one of your energetic signature, your state of being at the deepest level, the very essence of who you are as an energy field of patterns and relationships. Don't worry, I think you'll understand this more as we move along in the following chapters.

Now is the time to do it. Let's get that *shift* done.

So to start with...let's *shift* how we think about money. This is the first step to coming into money mastery.

CHAPTER FIVE

What Is Money Anyways?

Let's Take A Trip Back In Time.

Eons ago people exchanged goods and services in terms of a bartering system. *I'll give you this bag of grains and you give me your chicken.* Then people got the idea to use a substitute for the actual item that could reflect its value, like a gold coin, to make shopping easier in urban settings. (Imagine having to carry ten chickens to get your groceries.)

Eventually since gold and other metals were rather costly, a much cheaper mode for exchange purposes, like paper, started to be used which we've known for centuries as "money" but was to be "backed up" by gold and silver *in the past.*

So money really is just a piece of paper that has next to no intrinsic value. Its value lies in what it represents.

It's a *symbol* for the *perceived value* of the goods and services involved in any transaction. (Did you catch that…I said "perceived" value…that's why we have advertising campaigns, to convince us that certain items are of such and such a value.)

So when I go to work I am giving forth my value…my contribution to this world…and the value that I'm bringing to this world is being acknowledged by this piece of paper we call money in terms of a pay check. Then I go to the store and exchange something that I've created, by putting out my value in the world, to purchase things that other people have put out into the world that represents their value.

Now as soon as we're talking about value…the value that I bring to the world, that other people bring to the world, their services and the work that they do, the value that this planet brings to us in terms of resources, the ultimate source of all food and products that we have…we are talking about something ***sacred***.

The Sacredness Of Life.

Life is Sacred. Now what do I mean by that.

A sense of the sacred is tied to value. Ultimate value. What we deem as sacred is actually what we deem as being of the highest value, virtually priceless, irreplaceable, nothing else is like it. It's highly revered and treasured.

The reason this word has been associated with "religion" is because people viewed their experience of being connected with or contacting this highest reality we usually call "God" as being of the highest importance. Nothing is more important, is of greater value, than the divine. There's nothing else like "it".

Now let's think about life itself.

It's common for us to say that "life is sacred." Why? Because it's irreplaceable. There will never be another me or you. To be irreplaceable is to be priceless. Nothing can be bought to replace my life or yours.

Too often we stop there as though only human life is sacred. But let's not.

Let's extend that to see the truth that this applies to all of life, every minuscule element of it. That that particular tree, spider, cloud of that shape and movement, that particular raindrop…every tidbit of time and space…every passing moment of our experience…is unique and irreplaceable. It's about awakening to the inherent glorious beauty and wonder of life in any and every given moment! This is what it means to be enlightened.

When we live from that conscious awareness…of the priceless gift of life…we *shift*.

When we shift…all of our relationships shift.

Our relationship with others, our work, who we are, our lives as a whole. It all gets raised up to a higher level of meaning. Now we're getting into spirituality. An awakening of *awe* over the NOW, the present moment…a reverence for any and every given moment.

But let's keep it focused for our purposes here on how it relates to money and economics.

It's Time for a *Paradigm Shift!*

The outmoded vision behind economics today still operates from a merely pragmatic view. Where things have meaning and value in terms of how they *function* and in their position in a *cost-benefit analysis*. Their value is entirely **extrinsic**, that is, in their practical usefulness to others, how they can be *used*.

For example, the tree only has "meaning" or "value" in its function to provide me with shade on a hot day or the lumber to build my shed, i.e., what I can *use it for* in material terms. It's evaluated in terms of the cost in return for the benefit. All within the context of consumerism.

This is the consequence of our current *secular and consumerist* paradigm. Nature is viewed as inanimate, as "dead matter." In contrast to the ancients who viewed nature to be respected as alive and conscious. And therefore to be honoured and valued as such.

Secondly, this secularist paradigm is directed by the Darwinian model of competition, the survival of the fittest. The ethic that then determines the value of something is whether or not it enhances *our* survival. That we humans as the superior species has the right to exploit all others to serve our needs.

This paradigm leads to this *hierarchy* where those *in power* determine what is "practically useful" to them. So if it's practical for me to exploit children for slave labour, so be it. If it's to my benefit to slaughter sharks simply for their fins for a gourmet soup, so be it. If it's practical for me to send out soldiers as fodder in war, so be it. Where do we draw the line?

We get this massive global exploitation as depicted in the movie Avatar (check out John Perkins, *Confessions of an Economic Hit Man* and his YouTube interviews). Where the rich natural resources of the Amazonian jungle (where the powerless indigenous tribes live) can be cheaply gotten…stolen…and sold for millions…in the name of legitimate economic enterprise.

The problem is there's no higher ethic directing the economic enterprise other than how much something *costs* in order to get a higher return, or *benefit*, in dollars. Result: Massive exploitation.

Ironically, this very paradigm is undermining our survival. When we are so egocentrically driven to determine value according to our own benefit and our own minimal cost, it means "you have to lose in order for me to win." It fosters a cycle of destruction in the web of life.

But there's a catch.

I *need* you to live. We all are part of this larger eco-system that can only exist and be sustained through *inter-dependence*.

We need to reinvent the wisdom of our distant ancestors of pre-modern times. To shift our perspective from this utilitarian one, where we (as the superior, stronger species) define value in terms of pragmatic usefulness, to what I call **Sacred Abundance**. Seeing the *intrinsic* value in all of life that is to be honoured.

So going back to the example of the tree. That tree has intrinsic meaning and value tied to its unique beauty as that particular tree, and how it's in this amazing web of relations of give and take in the eco-system that supports the greater good of all life. It is a form of life to be respected and honoured as is all life.

Does that mean we are never to cut down a tree? Some may say so. Others would say that we can but to do so while honouring its value, doing so with caution and within conservationist policies. As indigenous people used to do, with prayer and appreciation for the gift of life that the tree would be offering. Recognizing the tree as the "one-legged" in a web of relations we humans have with all living beings.

Sacred Abundance

Coming to a place of honouring all life as sacred is the foundation for beginning to have a healthy, sacred relationship not just with money but with all of life. **It's all inter-related.** We seriously need to adopt this perspective of *Sacred Abundance* to secure a sustainable future for ourselves and this planet.

Now from this perspective -- where we operate from this sense of honouring the sacredness, the value of ourselves, others, and all the goods and services that we provide (thankfully due to this planet's resources) -- we could label this economic exchange as being a form of "divinity in action" a type of "holy exchange."

Linda Christensen, PhD

The web of life, this grand eco-system, is a divine dance of giving and receiving, of the exchanging of gifts that are meant to bless, nurture and serve each other.

This paradigm of *Sacred Abundance* if adopted can provide the ideal framework for how to live. It can give us our ethical map of "do's and don'ts." So seriously needed in today's economic practices that are simply directed by the ethic of utilitarianism with its one rule of making the most bucks with the least expense. This only leads to exploitation. Not only of resources but people. Life is devalued, simply translated into a dollar sign in the eyes of the exploiters, those in a position of power. The key problem is that that *money well* will eventually run dry. It just isn't self-sustaining.

A vision of *Sacred Abundance* can provide us with a life of meaning and purpose and the ethical guidelines that honours the value of others and life, with the end result being sustainability and the well-being of *all* life. That's the only way any form of abundance can be sustained.

So now with this larger framework in place, let's get into exploring where our money mindset is at!

CHAPTER SIX

What Does Money Mean To You?

It's time to do some exploring!

What sort of beliefs and ideas do you have around money? Let's find out.

(If you would rather do this exercise by following the audio instructions, get your free mp3 that you can download at MoneyMindsetShift.com.)

Exercise:

Get your pen and paper and let's do a bit of a free association exercise.

Step 1) Fill in the blank to the following statements *spontaneously*.

Now this is important…**don't think** about the answers…just quickly and briefly fill in the blanks with the first words or sentences that come to mind.

Don't worry about grammar, don't be analytical, be spontaneous. Just write the phrases, words, whatever comes up for you, in a brief and even messy way. Okay? Let's go.

(Do write out the following words like the beginning of a sentence that you're to complete.)

Money is….
Money is….
Wealth is….
Rich people are….
Rich people are….

The reason I can't become rich is....
The reason it's so hard for me to become rich is....
The reason I don't have enough money is....
The danger with getting rich is....
The problem with getting rich is....
The greatest fear I have about money is....
The greatest worry I have about money is....
The worst thing about money is....
Life is....
Work is....
I'm the kind of person who....
The problem with people is....
The problem with the world is....

Step 2) Now look at what's come up for you.
Ask yourself:
What sort of beliefs about money, about life, work, success, and about themselves, would a person be holding to in order to come up with such statements? Now really think about this.

Step 3) Get out a fresh sheet of paper and make two columns.
Heading on the left: *Current Limiting Beliefs*.
Heading on the right column: *New Empowering Beliefs*.

Now list the essence of the limiting beliefs you may be holding about money, life, success, your self in the left column. Come up with at least seven, if not ten.
 Keep this list handy as you go through the book! You'll get some insights along the way in terms of beliefs that you've been holding on to without realizing it. You'll be adding to this list as you read and things come up and get triggered.

Money Mindset Shift

In the right column, create a statement that would affirm the opposite, that which would be positive and empowering for you to replace the old belief. It would be something you would want to believe.

For example:

(Limiting Belief) The reason I can't become rich is…because nothing ever works out for me.

(Empowering Belief) Things always have an amazing way to work out for the best in my life.

Alright! So keep that handy and add to it as you go through the book.

Step 4) What you'll want to do is turn those new empowering beliefs into **daily affirmations** to reprogram yourself.

Write them out on index cards, repeat them into your phone as a recording to listen to daily. See them, hear them, and dream them by visualizing these new beliefs as being a part of your life.

Make it your intention to re-program yourself into those new, positive beliefs to replace the old negative ones.

Remember: the key to breaking through is to take action and implement!

Okay, so now you've got a bit of an idea as to where your money mindset is at, let's take a closer look at how our money mindset works.

CHAPTER SEVEN

Money Mindset: *It's all just in your head!*

Some years ago Donald Trump was worth 6 billion in terms of assets. He got himself into trouble and ended up being in debt by 900 million. Wow!

Within two and half years he got totally out of debt and got back his 6 billion plus some! WOW!!

How could he do that?

Donald Trump has a billionaire mindset.

His core being, his sense of identity, is one where he's a multi-billionaire. It didn't work for him to be 900 million in debt. He knew he could climb his way back out. This is what makes Trump…Donald Trump…it's part of his identity. It's his way of thinking, his way of operating in the world.

On the other hand, we've got the case of the majority of lottery winners who win millions but lose it all in a few years. They're five times more likely to end up filing for bankruptcy because they can't handle the wealth.

They don't have the right mindset in place and so they end up sabotaging themselves. Their money blocks show up and push the wealth away.

Fundamentally it's all about our money mindset. We've been conditioned and programmed to take on a whole body of beliefs and attitudes, a way of operating, habits and behaviours, that basically encompasses our money mindset.

So Where's Your Head At?

So here's our challenge. The vast majority of us have issues with money. If not money we'll have issues with our selves, life, success...basically how we show up in the world. You've probably seen that from the exercise you did in the last chapter. (You did do that exercise didn't you?)

These key things mess us up in our relationship with money. I'll be going through these in the following chapters but for now, let's find out some more as to where your head is at!

Exercise:

Here's a little exercise to find out where your ***money set point*** is at to see how much money you're comfortable allowing into your life. It's very simple.

Add up the total amount of money that's come to you in the past twelve months from all sources: income, inheritance, investments, through marriage, whatever....

Then divide it by twelve to get your monthly average.

That's your comfort zone, your money set point of comfort in terms of the amount of money you'll allow into your life without your reacting in panic or self-sabotage.

You see it's pretty basic.

> ***What we've got in our life is generally what we're pretty comfortable with.***

Even if it's miserable and impoverished.

I know that this can be hard to swallow initially. I had to learn all this the hard way.

Let me explain how this works.

From Money Mindset to Money Set Point

You see we're conditioned by our past experiences to accept certain things…to adapt, compromise, make it work…so we can cope with our situations. This results in *coping mechanisms*…patterns of behaviours, beliefs, emotional dynamics of how we manage life that sort of "work" for us. They become comfortable, familiar, feel safe to be in, even if they're not for our higher good.

This results in our having certain "set points" in every area of life in terms of what's comfortable and familiar to us. These are put in place as children and reflect the contexts we grew up in. So what we received and lived with as children in terms of affection, loving relationships (or not), money and provision (or not), successes and accomplishments (or not)…program us to feel safe and comfortable when we are in those similar contexts.

When we move out of them and experience wealth, success or intimacy on a different level -- we react. Like a thermostat that's set at a certain temperature. If the temperature rises, the air conditioner kicks in, if the temperature lowers, the heater kicks in.

So it is with us.

If the money is too low we get in gear and get a job, make the money to get back to what's comfortable. But if the money is so high, so foreign to us, we freak out and self-sabotage and energetically push it away so we drop back into our comfort zone.

This is what we need to understand:

Linda Christensen, PhD

> ***Whatever you are wanting***
> ***that is not in your life…***
> **in some way, at some level**
> ***is something you are resisting***
> ***and not allowing in.***

This is a basic Law of the Universe. A law based on resonance and how energy works. (Now of course, there are exceptions to this. Like living in a war torn country, where you're entangled in the collective consciousness and energy play at work.)

I know this can be hard to swallow when you first come across this. I rejected these sorts of ideas for years until I really got it that this is how it actually works.

Now before a guilt trip gets laid on you for this I want you to know this:

> ***We resist leaving our comfort zones out of fear.***
> ***That fear is a form of misguided self-love to protect***
> ***us from what's thought to be dangerous.***

We'll talk about this more in upcoming chapters. I just don't want you to start beating yourself up, judging and condemning yourself as a failure for having attracted a lot of lack and struggle into your life.

What's really going on is that little child in you that feels safe with what's familiar and believes it's in your best interest to stay put. And so he/she is keeping away changes that are felt to be potentially threatening. That includes more money and success in your life.

So the point here is that you've been programmed to only *allow* so much money to come into your life. This is where our money blocks come in.

Okay…so let's now explore these blocks one by one.

Part II

Uncovering Your Money Blocks

CHAPTER EIGHT

Money Block #1 - Fear

(aka *change is bad*)

Now fear is something we all struggle with. It's simply a part of our biology.

Think of when fear shows up in your life.

Isn't it when you're facing something different and new? Something that's about to change your life in some way?

Fear is an automatic biological reaction when we're entering into new territory, something different…the unknown…in a way that's outside of what we're normally comfortable with. (We talked a bit about this in the last chapter.)

Fear serves a purpose. Its intent is to protect us from potential danger.

When fear is triggered it's like an alarm bell going off that's meant to wake us up and be on *alert*. And so our adrenalin kicks in and we're ready for action…the fight or flight response.

This response comes from what's commonly called our reptilian brain or the amygdale.

It's a rather primitive part of the brain that's totally committed to the agenda of ensuring our safety and security. Keeping us safe from danger by warning us when we're venturing into new territory.

The Caveman Within

Imagine the caveman of old walking into an unknown part of the jungle...not knowing what's around the corner...his whole body's on red alert. So it is with us today. As soon as we enter the unfamiliar, a biochemical release of adrenalin kicks in and we experience fear, anxiety, doubt...getting us into a "red alert" mode. It's a natural, automatic biological reaction...just a part of our survival instinct serving to protect us.

In a nutshell...we're biologically wired to stick with what we know, to not venture into new horizons, to stay in the safety zone of the familiar.

Hence, our *resistance to change*.

So How Does This Show Up In Our Lives?

Here's what happens. We decide to take on something new...to change the direction of our life, enter into a new relationship, career, business venture...whatever...and fear and doubt shows up.

Our automatic reaction tends to be: "Oh no! This is *bad*, I'm feeling afraid...I'm not sure about this...it's a *warning* this isn't good for me!" And so we retreat back into our comfort zone of the familiar.

This often happens unconsciously. We might not realize that our putting off certain tasks is actually a way of bypassing the fears we have. We procrastinate so that we avoid feeling that fear. Yet we might not realize that's why we're procrastinating or start getting busy with other things that all of a sudden seem more important. It can be really sneaky!

End result: we stay stuck with the same old, same old.

We don't grow, we don't try new ventures, we don't stretch ourselves. We just dream our dreams but never realize them.

We end up living a small life and die with regrets. Wishing we had the guts to have tried different things…taken those opportunities that passed us by…followed through and completed those goals. But…it's too late.

Our Dreams Are On The Other Side!

We all have our different levels of what we can handle. We all have different boundaries as to how far we can or want to stretch ourselves. But we all eventually will hit that wall of fear that marks the line of where we're stepping into new territory. Especially if it means big changes will result, like a quantum leap breakthrough to a whole new level in our lives.

And guess what?

Our dreams are on the other side of that line. Just outside of our comfort zone.

Like a carrot on the stick.

Our dreams of what we'd love to all have, do and be. They're there. Calling us to cross over. To have courage, faith, some raw guts, to take that step into the unknown.

The catch is…that if we do it right…the bridge will appear to take us to our pot o'gold at the end of the rainbow.

Now that fear may not magically disappear.

That's what courage is about. To go forward despite the fear.

Linda Christensen, PhD

The Hero Within

There's some good news here.

We don't only have this primitive part of the brain that tries to keep us safe operating. We also have a grander part of us, the neo-cortex, this higher creative intelligence, that thrives on *novelty*.

And so we also have a biological impulse for growth, expansion, to be curious, eager to explore, to create, learn and do new things. This is what spurs our evolution, to actualize our higher potential.

We're also biologically wired to grow.

Our challenge is to use our intelligence to navigate this dance between the desire for growth and novelty and our resistance and fear of change, our unwillingness to let go of the familiar in order to move up to the next level. Below is an exercise and tips to empower you in this dance.

But first, let's understand this. Fear is meant to be our *ally*, not our enemy. We need to learn how to *work with it*.

When fear shows up, its intent is to protect us, it's letting us know we're leaving our safety zone. In other words, there's a part of us that's feeling we're taking on something that might not be safe for us and to proceed with caution. So be compassionate and kind to yourself.

Exercise:

So let's explore working with a fear.

Think of when you were a kid going on the roller coaster for the first time.

Money Mindset Shift

Yes…it was going to be scary. You felt the fear. But that bodily sensation can easily become excitement over the new adventure. It can be transmuted into eager anticipation.

That will be your goal here.

To transform your fears into allies that support you and have that energy become a source of empowerment and enthusiasm, passion and fire, instead of an energy that disempowers and blocks you.

Fear doesn't just go away. But it can start to transform into confidence as you make the new familiar through experience. You do that by taking it in baby steps where you can feel safe in venturing into this new territory and by having a positive attitude of eager anticipation.

Step 1) Pick something that you'd like to take on, a new venture that would be a step towards your dreams.

Step 2) Answer these questions:
Why haven't you done this yet? What's been holding you back? Are these just excuses to justify your not taking action? In what way are you not feeling safe in moving into this new venture?

Step 3) Do some journaling and inner exploration about this. Write non-stop without thinking about it, let your answers come spontaneously.

Just like in the previous exercise, fill in the blanks with the first words that come up for you. Just let it flow.

I'm afraid that...
I'm afraid of...
I'm afraid because...
I'm afraid if...

Step 4) Now make it safe for you. Put in place whatever you need to feel safe. Create a safety net for yourself. Talk to yourself and ask if these fears are real or mere conjecture. Assure your deeper self, the subconscious, the inner child, that you will make sure you've got the needed support and safety measures in place.

Step 5) Next, turn that fear into excitement, eager anticipation. You see, fear is a form of energy, an energy that gets your body ready to fight or run. You just need to transmute it into excitement and passion.

Step 6) Final point. When you're feeling like you just want to stay in your cozy cocoon, ask yourself — How can it get better than this? How can this even be better for me? Is it time for the butterfly to leave the cocoon and move into even better circumstances?

You see we fear **losing** the good we have when there's change. But if we see change as **adding** to the good we already have, we're more open and less resistant. If we take baby steps to gradually expand our comfort zones, and get comfortable with being uncomfortable, we can ***transform fear into passion.***

Now let's move on to the next block where we've inherited so many limiting beliefs around money.

CHAPTER NINE

Money Block #2 - Social Conditioning

(aka *money is bad*)

We've inherited all kinds of beliefs about money and wealth from society at large.
Check out this list of common sayings:

> Money is the root of all evil.
> Money corrupts.
> Rich people are greedy schmucks.
> Money doesn't grow on trees.
> You have to work hard for money.
> It takes money to make money.
> Money can't buy you happiness.
> It's just money…easy come, easy go.

Sound familiar? There are basically five key concepts, what I call *syndromes*, that mess us up.

- That I can't be spiritual and rich at the same time.
- There just isn't enough for everybody.
- Money corrupts you.
- Money is hard to come by.
- Money isn't important.

We'll go through these, one by one, so make note of which negative, limiting beliefs about money come up for you.

"I'm Spiritual Therefore I Can't Be Rich" Syndrome

We have this whole religious heritage that money is the root of all evil. What's happened is that spirituality and wealth have been polarized. You know, the whole idea that to be spiritual you have to be anti-materialistic. You either love God or money. In a nutshell, to be spiritual **and** wealthy is an oxymoron.

There's a lot of misguided thinking here. First off, the rationale behind spiritual traditions that call for the ascetic path of renouncing material desires and possessions was for a particular purpose.

That we don't look to material things to meet what's actually a spiritual need.

It's the human tendency to do that. And it's the guaranteed path to everlasting unhappiness.

Classic example: Shopping therapy.

You feel a bit depressed…and so you go to the mall on a shopping spree to perk yourself up.

Sure. You feel happy for that day or the next…but then you're back to feeling a bit low again, yet not too sure why.

Material things can't fill that whole inside.

That sense of emptiness, "lostness," loneliness. Those nagging questions of who am I, what's my life all about anyways. That hunger for something you don't quite know what to name. A hunger and longing that only goes away when you party and get high, or go shopping and get something new. This is actually a spiritual issue. It's pretty much what's behind all addictions. Addictions are essentially a spiritual problem needing a spiritual solution.

Getting to be really comfortable with who you are, knowing your deeper self, feeling at home in the Universe…that's what's needed. That's essentially a spiritual enterprise.

"Remember the Starving Children in Africa" Syndrome

I'm sure you've heard this one as a kid. "Now clean up your plate! Think of all the starving children in the world. We don't waste food around here."

Many of us have inherited a scarcity mentality from parents who went through The Great Depression during the war years. Having grown up with having to penny pinch all the time, never to waste anything. Being told "That's enough now, you don't need more than that. Be thankful you have at least that."

What's been imprinted upon us, and modelled for us, are two things.

First, that *there isn't enough to go around*, that **scarcity** is the name of the game of life.

Out of fear of not having enough we become hoarders, afraid of letting go, of giving away too much, a fear that we won't get it back. It's assumed abundance doesn't exist and it's hard to ever have enough. This creates a resistance to any kind of investing that might involve some risk, along with a great payback.

Linda Christensen, PhD

We tend to stay small and live small as we avoid any risk of losing the little that we have.

I read this story of an old man who was known for going through everyone's garbage, lived in a hovel, and looked like a street person even though he wasn't homeless. When he died they found over $100K stuffed away in the walls of his house. So he wasn't actually poor, but his hoarding mindset was a poverty stricken one. The result…he lived in poverty despite having money. To live in constant self-deprivation reflects a poverty consciousness.

Yes, it's true that you can't take it with you. So do enjoy your abundance! That's the whole point of it. Life is filled with treasures we're meant to enjoy!

Second, that we must bear some **guilt** if we're not impoverished. We're made to *feel guilty if we are abundant* and have more than enough! That *that* is somehow bad.

For example, when we were kids and didn't want to finish our plate even though we're full…we got this major shaming session.

Why are we to feel bad? To feel guilty?

Because it's assumed that what we have was somehow taken from someone else and therefore if I have enough it's at the price of someone else being deprived. Why?

Because there isn't enough to go around! Supplies are limited. There isn't enough food in the world.

We've been conditioned to think it's unreasonable to believe that everyone can have what they want!

Now is that the truth? Is that the real problem?

Isn't the problem more of a political one, in terms of a lack of effective systems in place to allow for both

Money Mindset Shift

better food distribution and elimination of waste? The food that gets wasted in restaurants is astronomical. Buffets aren't allowed to keep and re-serve the food that was available on display for "safety" reasons. (Watch the Ted talk by Tristram Stuart on The Global Food Waste Scandal.) Is it really that we should just not buy anything and live strict minimalist lives? What if we all just went through life scraping by, not buying anything, making do with very little…how many people would become jobless as a result? How many businesses would shut down?

One thing we need to realize is that the vast majority of businesses are small to medium, family owned and the very source of their livelihood to put bread on the table. Few are the mega corporations that exploit the third world and our natural resources.

I call it Scare-City.
Our whole mindset has been conditioned into this "there's not enough to go around" paradigm.

The flip side of this "Scare-City" paradigm of there not being enough is that we have to fight for the little that there is. To survive you have to outdo the competition, for me to win means you have to lose. It can't be win-win because there just isn't enough for everybody. It's all about a survival of the fittest. This is the major drive behind political conflicts and outright war.

Of course we shouldn't waste and squander. Yes we do seriously need to address the systems in place that result in the paradox of *massive waste alongside poverty*. But also, let's expand our perspective on this. It's a matter of honouring both myself and food. Not taking things for granted, not being lazy and just chucking everything in the garbage, but being creative and frugal. BUT the key thing is to do this from a place, a state of being, a consciousness, that's not rooted in fear and scarcity, nor in mindless gluttony and extravagance but in **sacred abundance**.

Imagine if we operated from a paradigm of co-operation, collaboration, a win-win philosophy, that we all together can come into abundance if we work together. What would be possible for us if we operated from this perspective? That's the paradigm we have to shift into if we're going to make it on this planet.

"Money Just Makes You Greedy" Syndrome

We've also been conditioned to feel that anyone out to make money has to be exploitive, deceptive, and manipulative in order to do the sell job. Whereas anyone with sincere motives works at the food bank.

We're wary of people trying to rip us off in sales, or of getting into any new business venture. We tend to think that anybody who has a desire for success and wealth is at heart a greedy, material (unenlightened) beast. Now I'm not going to claim that greedy people don't exist…but let's get this straight, money isn't the culprit. Greedy people are greedy people just as generous people are generous.

Money isn't the problem. Money itself is neutral, it's a tool, like a knife. It only becomes certain things in the hands of the user…to slice some bread or to slice up people.

Money only amplifies who you already are.

Money Mindset Shift

So if you're a generous person, money opens the gates of your generosity.

If you're a miser, money allows you to hoard even more of it.

If you're a greedy schmuck, money just allows you to go and be even a greater greedy schmuck!

It's not money's fault. It's all up to you. Who do you choose to be? How do you choose to live? What are your plans for that money you want to bring into your life?

"Money Doesn't Grow On Trees" Syndrome

We've all heard this one. The whole idea that you have to work hard for money.

Yes, we do need to work. We do need to put in that effort in some way. Does it have to require slave labour? Of course not. Does it have to be ongoing struggle? No.

There are many ways of making money. These days more than ever we can be smart about it. Leverage our resources, make use of other people's money, talent, time...and create a channel for money to flow through.

Another mindset shift is called for here. We need to think of creating *money channels*. Not just our physical labour to get paid by the hour. It's about directing energy, being a manager of money streams, and there are many ways to do it other than the basic direct line of dollar per hour wage.

You see life is a tapestry of diversity that together creates this beautiful piece of art, this eco-system web of life. Like a puzzle, everyone has a place to fit in, a contribution to make that fits and suits that individual. For some, getting that job at minimum wage works for them, it fits with their skill set. Not everyone is suited to become a millionaire.

It's not about just having that money, it's about who you all are.

You need to BE a millionaire in order to create and manage that amount of money. There has to be a resonance, a fit, between who you all are with that amount of wealth. You have to step into your greatness to play that bigger game.

If it doesn't fit, then life is inviting you to grow and learn, move past your fears and take on higher levels of bringing your value into the world. What many do is just let themselves stay stuck, gripe and complain about their crappy job and blame the economy, their parents, those rich people…whatever.

But pathways of possibilities exist.

If the desire is there, there is a way.

That desire reflects your life's calling in some way. You can be guided on that pathway through your connection with God/Source/Universe, that higher reality will provide whatever support you need for your situation. There's a lot involved with this, in terms of integrity, authenticity, motivation.

In the paradigm I advocate here of sacred abundance, the motivation is to be of service and to be in alignment with your sense of calling and life purpose. Then true abundance, enlightened wealth, can come your way, of having more than enough with fulfillment and joy.

"It's Only Money" Syndrome

For many today, and especially for the younger generation, there's a trend of not valuing and appreciating money. It's also an issue for those who've inherited wealth. There's a sense of entitlement, that money comes easily. This is a generation that grew up in the affluent years created by and enjoyed by their baby boomer parents. They pretty much got whatever and whenever they wanted.

The result: Money isn't treasured and honoured, but is taken for granted. It's neglected and undervalued.

You hear this in how people talk about money, saying things like…

"It's *only* money."

"I *only* have 20 bucks on me."

" I *only* make two grand a month."

To regard money in terms of "*only*" devalues it instead of honouring it.

The youth of today are also growing up in a cashless society. As talked about earlier, we're now so disconnected from money. It's just a number being transferred without any sense of what it takes to earn it. Debt is skyrocketing. Money is too easy to get in terms of credit and loans, a huge issue for college students. After graduating they can't get enough cash together for a down payment for a house. In fact, most of them still live with their parents, crippled by this huge debt from going to college and still not able to get a job!

Exercise:

Pull out your list of beliefs around money from the exercise you did in Chapter 6. Go through these syndromes again and write down what sort of beliefs

Linda Christensen, PhD

have influenced you in these areas in your column of limiting beliefs.

Now in the other column write out the opposite belief that can be an empowering affirmation to support you in shifting your mindset around money and success.

Let's now take a look at another money block that shows up for most people...the "woundings" of life.

CHAPTER TEN

Money Block #3 - Woundings

(aka *life is bad*)

The Woundings of Life

Life isn't always fair and things don't always go as planned. We get wounded by life. Having hurtful experiences around money that leaves scars.

You've heard the stories…of how friends, family and spouses can become your worst nightmare.

So many men worked hard to create a successful business only to hand it over to their ex. Family feuds over inheritances, siblings not speaking for years or even suing each other, getting ripped off by former business partners.

Greed runs rampant.

Then for others, business failure is the wound. You've heard the stat on this that over time virtually 90% of small businesses fail. How many these days have had to file for bankruptcy and lose everything.

All this effort, all the work of trying to create something of a business, to get ahead in life, only to be left with the shirt on your back. What's the point of all this effort when there's no payback?

We can be left devastated from such experiences, deeply wounded by life. Feeling despair over moving forward and starting over. So you become cynical about success, making money, being ambitious.

Here we need to remember the following.

Failures Are the Stepping Stones to Success

Failures and obstacles are the stepping stones to success. If you look at the track record of the successful you find that these experiences are part of the package on the road to success. Virtually every big player has stories of business failure, being cheated, sued, having gone bankrupt.

The catch is…they didn't let this stop them.

They got back in the saddle and moved forward. They take the **negative** experience for a **learning** experience. Transforming the wall, the obstacle, the dead end, into a stepping stone on the road to success.

This is life.

It's not perfect. It's not always fair. There are tough times. May these be taken as growing pains to expand your being, expand your awareness, so you become wiser and more capable.

Life is our greatest teacher, inviting us to become bigger than our problems.

Commit to being unstoppable.

Exercise:

Exploration time! Get out that pen and paper. Ask yourself these questions:

1) What are some of my life wounds? How may they have left me wary, gun-shy, hesitant to move forward into new ventures?

2) Do I want to stay stuck here with this? Am I willing to move forward again? If so, when?

3) What would moving forward look like? What actions would I take?

4) Who and what do I need to forgive? Do I need to forgive myself, God, Life? What can I let go of now?

5) What have I learned from my challenging experiences? How can these lessons now serve and empower me?

6) How can I protect myself and avoid the same thing happening in the future? How can I safely pick up the broken pieces and once again launch my dream but wiser and better prepared to take it to success?

Not only do we get hurt by these experiences, and probably feel that life is out to get us, they also can deeply impact our sense of self-worth. This is the next block to deal with and it's the most potent of them all.

CHAPTER ELEVEN

Money Block #4 -

Low Self-Worth (aka *I am bad*)

We now go from the idea that somehow money is bad, business is bad, success is bad, life is bad…to the idea that *I am bad.*

I've been amazed over how many of my various clients were blocked over this issue…a sense of unworthiness, of not deserving wealth and success, abundance and prosperity, all the good that life has to offer.

It's pandemic.

Virtually every human being struggles with this issue of unworthiness.

The effect of this is that we end up *rejecting abundance* because we don't really believe or feel that we actually *deserve it.*

How Often Were You Told "No" versus "Yes"

A lot of this has its roots in early childhood where we were raised to believe that we cannot have what we want. And to seek what we want…to try to get what we want…is seen as selfish and wrong.

We'd be punished for what we'd want to do. Judged and condemned…told that it's stupid, or selfish, somehow wrong or bad.

Linda Christensen, PhD

It's estimated that by the time you're 17 you were told "No, you can't" 150,000 times. In contrast, on average, you were told "Yes, you can" only 5,000 times.

Just think of what you were all told as a kid.

No, you can't do this...you can't do that.
No, that's not right...that's not good.
Quit being so stupid, so clumsy, so thoughtless, so selfish.
You should do this instead...do what your teacher tells you to do...listen to me...do as I say.
Be more like your sister...be more considerate of what others want.... On and on it goes.

Basically we're conditioned to do things to make our parents, our teachers, our friends, our spouses, our bosses...you name it...**other people**...even God...happy. That is, to *not* do what **you** want, to *not* be who **you** really are, but to conform to other's agendas.

The bottom line message we get is...

It's not okay to be me. I don't have the right to do what I want for my own happiness and well being.

So the result of this is that we disconnect from who we really all are. We then don't even know what we want. We constantly doubt ourselves and don't ever find our true genius that we're meant to bring into the world. That special gift where we shine our unique brilliance.

So we end up staying small and we don't **activate our worth**. All because we've never been encouraged or affirmed, never given permission to shine our light, to step into our own greatness, to be who we all want to be...and *are meant to be by design*...on our terms.

This is what seriously needs to be addressed and turned around.

Shine Your Light!

We are meant to bring our unique gifts, talents, very presence, to the world. And the desires we have are actually the voice of our souls to bring forth those gifts, talents, abilities into this world.

You see our desires represent (when uncontaminated) our *core energy*, and that energy is part of our *life essence*. So if my energetic DNA, so to speak, is one where I have a gift for music or math, I will naturally have a desire for engaging those, it brings me pleasure, a sense of fulfillment. I will be pushed from within, energetically in the form of desire, to long to do those things.

Life, that which we are a particular expression of, is by nature expansive. It has a design and order that's in harmony with the larger ecosystem, a system of give and take that benefits the Life Process as a whole. Its impulse is to be expressed, to manifest, to actualize its potential. And for us, it's to shine our unique essence, our light and then to be blessed in return as we are giving out our gift to others.

Then we receive the reward and appreciation from others for our gifts. As we enjoy and celebrate other's being-ness…they in turn enjoy and celebrate ours. It's the grand gift of life! This planet and all its amazing life forms are to be appreciated and honoured as we enter into a sacred relationship with it. A circle of joy and beauty. This is truly a *"Circle of Life"* (Lion King).

That's what's meant to be.

But what happens for many is a *Circle of Despair* gets activated.

If you believe that you have nothing good to offer, you feel small, like a "nobody" and so you don't shine any light of YOU. Instead you passively go through life allowing the outer world and others dictate what and how you should be. The end result is your life has minimal impact, minimal gifting. It becomes a self-fulfilling prophecy. You don't feel you are worthy, you don't offer anything much of worth, and so your life seems worthless. Why?

Because you never activated your worth.

This is key. This is what life is about and what our purpose is. We are to *activate your worth*. Know our worth, discover, explore and express it in the world. As we do…life will give us the feedback and affirm the fact of our worthiness.

Exercise:
Every night before going to bed, during your nightly ritual of brushing your teeth, washing your face, whatever it is that you do…look in that bathroom mirror and say to yourself "(Your name), I love you, you are wonderful, and I appreciate who you all are. I want to acknowledge you for what you all did today…."

Then go through the various things you did that day that was good, from the mundane of having gotten out of bed and fed yourself, to having closed a mega-deal in business. Whatever that fits with where you're at in your life. Take a moment to *affirm your value*. Be in gratitude for YOU, who you are, as well as all the good things in your life.

Word of warning though!

When you are in a *state of despair* what will want to show up is a *shaming session* of all the things you did **not** do, of how you failed, and how disgusted you are with yourself.

You've got to turn this around.

Commit to starting a new cycle of affirmation and worthiness, of hope and renewal. That starts with stopping the negative self-talk and committing to making the change, to getting your life on a positive track. It can be done…with the help of your Higher Power. Pray and ask for that support. It works.

Now we'll move on to the last money block. How we tend to live in clutter and disorganization often as a way to avoid coming into full power.

CHAPTER TWELVE

Money Block #5 - Money Chaos

(aka *order is bad*)

It's All About Energy

A key idea I work with in all of this is that life is a dance, an inter-play of energy.

What I mean by that is that the nature of reality consists of various patterns of how things relate. That pattern of relationship is actually a dynamic of energy, a type of signature of how things are positioned to each other that carries a particular pattern, a dynamism of interaction and connection.

As a pattern it propels things in a certain direction with a particular momentum. That pattern can either be in resonance with other similar patterns and is therefore receptive to those things, or it can repel other energy patterns. This is what's meant by all the talk about "the law of attraction" and "matching vibrational frequencies."

What Chaos and Clutter are REALLY all About

When our lives are cluttered and in chaos, there's usually a corresponding chaos in our finances and home.

When things are in disarray, disorganized, a mess…we'll be scattered, unclear, confused, and running in circles going nowhere. On the treadmill, exerting all this energy and effort but just staying put.

So when we have a lot of stuff…things we don't use regularly but hold on to in case we might need them someday…we are living from fear and scarcity. In hoarding things we're trying to feel secure. We don't want to let things go out of fear we'll be left with nothing.

Not only that, chances are…now get this…*we're afraid to truly be in alignment with our purpose,* to seriously get on with it in our lives.

Clutter hides us from our truth.

Clutter is the big distractor we put in place. Why? We're afraid of being fully present to ourselves. To seriously face the challenge of how we're showing up in the world. It functions to cloud our vision so we have an excuse not to step into our greatness and own our power…all on a subconscious level. Explore this one. Take some time to meditate on it.

What are you really avoiding by giving yourself the excuse of being busy with all your stuff? Not being organized enough to actually get ahead? What are you afraid of?

Money Mess Blocks the Flow

Now specifically with money, we need to bring things into order.

When we're cluttered and in a "money mess" we're blocking the flow of money in our lives. We'll experience *money guck*. Like a clogged drain full of sludge that doesn't allow the water to flow, so with our money.

Ask yourself, do you…

- know what you're making
- what you're spending
- what your debts are
- have a savings plan
- have important paper work that can't be found
- have bills scattered around
- not paid on time
- not accounted for
- have money itself scattered and not accounted for
- have your finances in a mess?

If so, money will not be happy in your home. It's not being cared for, nurtured, welcomed. It's like an abandoned puppy! I know this sounds corny but you'd be amazed at the transformation if you started to treat your money as a person, a living being.

Fall in love with money!

Nurture and caress it, enjoy and appreciate it, create this excitement and joyful expectancy around money. You've got to *shift* that energy so you *attract* it!

Poor money habits and not knowing how to manage it effectively blocks abundance from our lives. If we don't track our income, don't track our expenses, don't pay our bills on time, don't know what our assets and liabilities all add up to, are in a debt cycle, don't have a clue as to how to create a wealth cycle…all this blocks money from flowing into our lives.

These all make up a behaviour pattern that indicates a neglect and fear of money, which results in an energetic disconnect from money.

That translates as a relationship that *repels* money.

Exercise:

Step 1) Commit to taking one hour this week to create a file for all your bills, mortgage and bank statements, insurance policies, taxes…all the paper work that involves your money coming in and going out.
I use an accordion file so all the financial stuff is in one place but also in separate categories.
Get it all organized! It's really not that hard.

Step 2) Start the habit of recording your expenses and income daily. Track your money. Give it some loving attention.

Step 3) If you have debt commit to a debt pay-off plan. List the credit cards, with the amounts owed, the interest charged and the minimum monthly payments. Know your numbers. Next pick the one with the highest interest to pay off first and put an extra amount towards it every month. And, most importantly, stop the cycle of increasing your debt. Cut up your cards if you have to. See if you can get a line of credit at a lower interest rate. Phone your credit card companies and ask for a lower rate. You've got to turn this around. When you start seeing results you'll be inspired to keep it up.

Step 4) Now think of what you'd like to do with some extra money. What trips would you like to make? Things you'd like to buy? Amazing experiences you'd like to have?

Money Mindset Shift

List these. Estimate the cost involved. Create a vision board and start to anchor energy around what you want to use that money for through feeling the joy of realizing those dreams. Declare the destiny for your money.

Step 5) Now explore and invite the possibilities of that extra income coming to you as you find ways to bring your value into the world. Create channels for money to flow to you (its entrance). You've created the channels in this list of where the money will flow from you (its exit). Money is meant to circulate, to receive and give. You are now beginning to turn the tide to enter into abundance.

Just as you create energetic anchors for where the money is to go, you likewise create energetic channels through which that money will come. It's all about working that energy through your mind in terms of visualizations and emotions in terms of your feelings of expectancy, enthusiasm and confidence.

To help you with this get your bonus "Track Your Treasures" Sheet, at MoneyMindsetShift.com, use the code MONEYSHIFT.

Now we come to the grand finale!
What all these money blocks add up to is a bad contract we've got going on between ourselves, life, and money. This is the energetic pattern or dynamic at play that brings you the correlating results.

CHAPTER THIRTEEN

What This All Adds Up To Is...

A Bad Money Contract

You see all these beliefs, "woundings," and conditioning we've been subject to create a particular energetic grid within us that defines our relationship with not just money but life in general.

We already talked about this.

Energetic patterns that were created by our past beliefs, emotions, experiences (and how we've integrated them), our environment (the energetic impact of people and things close to us) and our biological and cultural heritage.

Now the catch is this. These patterns operate like a *story*…the story of our lives. A story we've created that interprets our experiences in alignment with particular beliefs.

We've Forged Some Bad Contracts

This story pattern is actually a type of *spiritual commitment* we've made. It functions like a **contract**, a type of vow, an agreement we've entered into about how life works, how money works, and where we fit into the picture. These beliefs form a pattern, a type of *dynamic,* a particular interplay of energy, which is what all relationships essentially are.

Because we're so living *in* "our story" we're usually blind *to* it. It's unconsciously operating and we're like a pawn in the playing out of that story. So it all becomes this self-fulfilling prophecy.

Help! Get Me Outa Here!
Our stories are like this box that we're in that we can't really get a perspective on because we're inside of that box.

Nevertheless, these stories or patterns by default continue to shape how and who we are and our experience of life…if we remain unaware and passive.

So the *bad news* is that a lot of us are caught up in some limiting, negative stories that basically are bad contracts we've committed to. As we live from and within these stories we create a life that reflects those stories. That's what's meant by the popular saying "you create your reality."

The *good news* is that we can undo those old contracts and stories and create new ones and in doing so create a new life.

But wait…there's more.

Help! I'm Surrounded by Stories.
Okay…we've talked a lot about *our* having these stories…but that's not the whole story! We're also living out *other people's stories.*

The world around us…from society at large to individuals…also live out their stories! Academics often refer to "culture" as a "cult" in that any given culture embeds into our psyches a set of beliefs and expectations. Everybody has their agenda operating that dictates how they chose to relate to us.

They'll have their story about who they think *you* are! They'll have their boxes that they'll put *you* in.

We're like this billiard ball being knocked around on the table of life by the cues of others, various forces and factors outside of us. But not only do others have mastery over us. So do events and circumstances.

We too readily allow things like being in an accident, getting laid off, going through an economic downturn, having an illness, whatever…dictate our state of being. We create a *story* around these things to justify our experience of limitation, lack of success, and unhappiness.

Then we also tend to play out the larger story operating in any given society. If it's being an American, a Palestinian, Jew, or Jihadist, wherever people hold to nationalistic, ethnic or religious identities. In fact any sense of "identity" is tied to a "story." People chose to *attach* to such identities unconsciously, as a given, due to birth and indoctrination.

It's time to seriously wake up and question the validity of these stories, especially when they lead to ongoing violence, suffering and misery.

"Those who don't have power over the story that dominates their lives, the power to retell it, rethink it, deconstruct it…and change it as times change, truly are powerless because they can't think new thoughts."
Salman Rushdie

Exercise:
Do some journaling and reflecting around these questions:

What sort of stories have been running your life?

Do you strongly attach to a particular religious or ethnic identity?

How about an identity associated with certain events or experiences?

How might these stories and identities be limiting you?

What's the price of staying with them, being stuck in them?

What might they be keeping from you what you really want in life?

What might they be bringing into your life that really isn't serving you?

Is it time to let any of them go?

What bigger story can you take on that would be more empowering for you?

Think of the various things you'd like to see in your life, things you'd like to experience, do, have and be. What would be your ideal life?

What kind of story about who you are and what life is about would support your having that ideal life?

So this leads us to the ultimate question in life! The conclusion that ultimately reveals that our journey to master money and come into prosperity and abundance is indeed a spiritual journey!

CHAPTER FOURTEEN

So What's Your Story Going To Be?

Our bigger story about life is intimately connected with, and actually a reflection of, what we actually believe about ourselves. This will be the rudder that steers our lives. And so the ultimate question is...

Who Do You Want To Be?
The perennial question life invites us to explore: who am I?
- What do you believe about "who you are?"
- How does that shape and direct your life?
- Are you happy with the results?
- Are you sure you don't want to question that?

As a whole, if we remain unconscious and passive...life happens *to* us. We end up playing out everyone else's stories, their dramas and agendas, taking them on as our own.

At what price? Your soul! You are giving your life over to *them* if you remain unconscious and passive.

It doesn't have to be this way. Especially since most of these patterns and stories aren't leading to the best that life can offer.

When we're suffering and experience struggle in life look at it as an invitation to wake up to whatever stories are operating. See it as an invite from the Universe to own your power, to come into mastery over your life. To consciously and proactively create what you want.

To be who and how you want to be. We do create our realities in terms of our personal lives.

This is the amazing capacity that we humans have that so sets us apart from other species. Our ability and requirement to create our sense of self. But far too often our vision is too low of who and what we can all become.

We do need models to inspire us of those who've attained a higher level of life mastery. Here I do think the history of religion and spirituality provides us with some examples.

The best ones in my mind are Jesus of Nazareth (aka the Christ) and Siddhartha Gautama (aka the Buddha). They show us what may be possible. The history of religion is full of examples of people approaching this mastery.

They transcend puny egocentric identities. They've awakened to an identity that's shifted from a *me* to a *we*.

When that happens you live from love and compassion for all of life. There's no longer any basis for division rooted in particular ethnic or religious identities.

Now when you think of it, what is it that really makes a business successful? Any person successful for that matter?

Isn't it when they are truly committed to serving others, when the collective good of all is their primary commitment? That they actually serve the needs of the people, the planet, and are creatively contributing to the larger welfare of life and leave a legacy?

Doing that brings not only the experience of material success but personal success in terms of a sense of peace, deep satisfaction and fulfillment, of having lived with meaning and purpose. When you think of

Money Mindset Shift

what abundance all means, the bottom line would be a sense of being full, of "enoughness".

Enough peace and contentment, joy and love, connection and meaning. Of not hungering or longing for something more or something else. A sense of completeness of being in the here and now yet with the sense of gratification of purposeful connection with Life. Blissful service.

Authentic success and abundance in life can only truly come when we leave the world a better place, we've given and contributed to the well-being of others. This is the fundamental nature of Life itself as this amazing eco-system, of give and receive, a "Circle of Life" that displays Sacred Abundance.

This is the context that we need to position our relationship to money in. As we position our quest for success as service to the world, activating our worth, bringing forth our unique giftings and talents, we are creating true wealth. We've then manifested our value into the world in a deep and powerful way.

Now For The Best Kept Secret!

The real power to access abundance and to live a life of freedom and joy is in knowing the true Source of all Abundance. To live connected with that Source, having that be the basis of one's being, where the "self" as "I," as this particular biological entity as "Linda Christensen," is grounded in, has a sense of identity with, the Source of all Life, the Ground of all Being, God, the Universe, whatever term you want to use.

This is why money mastery is actually a part of the spiritual journey! It involves an awakening of one's deeper identity and power to *shift* reality. To come into this creative partnership with the Universe. To enter into a spiritual agreement, a contract of *blessing*, not curse. Of *abundance*, not poverty. Of *joy*, not misery. Of *flow*, not struggle. Of *love*, not fear. Of *service* and *generosity* not miserliness and greed. Of *receiving* and *gratitude* not demanding entitlement.

I believe that abundance is meant to be our destiny and success is to be our life mission. We are called to live from a higher paradigm that ennobles the economic enterprise by contextualizing it as a holy exchange of sacred value that enhances the well-being of all, contributing to the larger eco-system of life that we're all a part of.

Right now we're on a path of destruction and exploitation that cannot be sustained. It's an attack on LIFE itself. We need a higher vision of *why* we do *what* we do that can govern our *how's* of doing.

As individuals we may feel powerless to change the world, yet we're all in this dance of life, trying to make a living. Change begins with us, in how we operate in our everyday lives.

Let's make the *Shift* to a new paradigm, a new *story*, one of Sacred Abundance.

Let's heal ourselves of past woundings and low self-worth.

Let's set ourselves free from limiting and negative beliefs that disempower and misdirect us.

Let's own our power and get our lives in order, on track, on purpose.

Let's take action despite our fears and not be held back and remain small.

Let's step *up* and *into* our inherent greatness and activate our worth and bring our value, and the richness of who we all are as individuals, into the world for the benefit of all.

Please join me in manifesting the true meaning of wealth. The world needs it.

I hope you found this book of value and that it effected some transformation, and made your life *richer* in having read it. If so, then I succeeded in part to manifest my wealth in having brought value into the world, into your life, in writing this for you.

Please share any stories of breakthrough with me, I would love to hear about it to know that in some way through this book, I've *activated my worth*. I'd be thrilled. Just email me Linda@YesYourLife.com

Thank you for spending this time with me and I look forward to future connections with you.

About The Author

Having been raised in a non-religious home, Linda got on the spiritual path as a result of life-changing spiritual experiences. This led her to the study of religion, a journey of attaining two master's degrees and a PhD in that area. Her journey was one of being led into religion, through religion, to then go beyond religion, to deconstruct the whole human quest in more universal terms. Having to make the journey herself from being "so spiritual to not give any attention to the material" and living in rather impoverished conditions most of her adult life, led to a wake-up call in revisiting what authentic spirituality and authentic success actually entail. The end result is an integration of the two in what she terms "Sacred Abundance."

This is the beginning of her work in forging a paradigm shift that involves decoding what religion is actually all about and understanding the whole dance of life in terms of *energy*. This is the first in a series of Success Power Books.

Forthcoming are *Intuition Knows: How to Use the Power of Intuition to Get Guidance, Clarity and Inspiration for Life Success*; *Prosperity Power: The 12 Essential Principles to Map Your Road to Success*, and *On Being Spiritual: A Five Step Process for Daily Practice*.

A best-selling author, Dr. Linda Christensen has been interviewed on CBC TV, Global TV, and the Bill Goodman Show. A former radio host herself she's also the co-founder of Conscious Living Radio in Vancouver. She regularly conducts workshops on spirituality and abundance and is a Money and Success Coach helping her clients to align their purpose with money and business to become successful, conscious entrepreneurs. She's taught for over 25 years at the university and college level in comparative religion and is passionate about integrating spirituality with success and decoding the deeper meaning of both. A single parent for 12 years, a lover of tennis, volleyball and dancing, she lives with her son in Vancouver, Canada.

This book and all her work is part of her personal mission to be a channel for bringing joyful abundance to others.

Go to **MoneyMindsetShift.com** to access your bonuses, including an audio version by using the code MONEYSHIFT.

AND

Special Invite!

Would love to have you join an upcoming
40 Day MoneyShift Challenge!

This is an online course with various webinars and handouts, live Q & A sessions, and powerful tools, where you'll be led through various exercises and daily practices to start shifting your energetic relationship with money.
Make sure to be on the list to get notified when a new session starts by emailing Linda@YesYourLife.com!

Printed in Great Britain
by Amazon